For *Harold* & *Connie*,
who introduced me to Shaks.

~*MR*

hakespeare

His Work & His World

Michael Rosen
Illustrated by Robert Ingpen

CANDLEWICK PRESS
CAMBRIDGE, MASSACHUSETTS

Liberty! Freedom! Tyranny is dead!
Run hence, proclaim, cry it about the streets.

Julius Caesar / 3.1 / Lines 77–8

Contents

IT'S THE MIDDLE OF THE NIGHT ON THE EDGE OF LONDON, A FEW DAYS AFTER CHRISTMAS DAY 1598. THE RIVER THAMES IS FROZEN OVER. SNOW IS FALLING. The roofs of the timbered houses and the nearby fields are white with it. Four buildings stand

A PLOT!

higher than the nearby houses, shops, bowling alleys, gambling houses, and taverns — a windmill, a church, and two theatres. One of the theatres is called the Curtain, and the other simply the Theatre. They are tall wooden buildings that have been there for only ten years or so, but in that time their walls have shaken to the sound of swords clashing in fencing matches, actors crying of murder or lost love, and audiences roaring with laughter. But tonight sixteen men are pulling down the Theatre. Two of them are brothers. They run a company of actors who put on plays, and with them are a builder and his workmen. As the men hurry about their work, it's clear that what's going on is secret and must be done as quickly as possible.

The Theatre

The Curtain

Through the night the workmen load timbers onto wagons. Two strangers arrive and start quizzing them. The workmen lie and say they are taking down only the parts of the building that are decaying. Really, they are dismantling the whole theatre and taking it somewhere else. It's a risky business because if it can be proved that they are stealing, they will all be hanged and their severed heads put on show. But before long the men are taking the timbers across London Bridge to Southwark, where the theatre will be rebuilt and become known as one of the world's most famous theatres: the Globe.

1598

Those two theatres on the edge of London were where the first plays of William Shakespeare were put on. But Shakespeare wasn't the kind of writer who sent off his plays and sat around hoping someone might perform them. He was an actor who worked in the same company as those men who dismantled the Theatre, and what's more, he was one of the new owners of the Globe.

In the four hundred years since then, he has become one of the world's most famous writers.

London →

So how does someone stay that famous? This is like asking another question:

What's So Special About Shakespeare?

Watching Shakespeare's plays is like being invited into a house full of amazing rooms. Go through a door at the top of the house and you will meet a ghost walking the battlements of a castle at night. You will hear him telling a young man that he is the ghost of his father, the old king. What's more, the ghost reveals that he was murdered by his own brother. And then the ghost says:

If thou didst ever thy dear father love —
Revenge his foul and most unnatural murder.

Hamlet / 1.5 / Lines 23, 25

What will the young man do?
Walk into one of the rooms and you will come
across a rich man yelling at his daughter because
she won't marry the man he has chosen for her. He shouts:

An you be mine, I'll give you to my friend.
An you be not, hang, beg, starve, die in the streets . . . {*an = if*}

Romeo and Juliet / 3.5 / Lines 191–2

But the girl has secretly married another man. What's going to happen? Move along into another room and a group of men are whispering amongst themselves. They are dressed in the clothes of ancient Rome and they are working out how they are going to murder the future king:

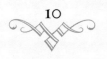

. . . And, gentle friends,
Let's kill him boldly, but not wrathfully.
Let's carve him as a dish fit for the gods,
Not hew him as a carcass fit for hounds.

Julius Caesar / 2.1 / Lines 171–4

Will they do it? If they do, will they get away with it?

And out in the garden of the house, a bunch of crazy people have come up with a great practical joke. They've tricked a stuffy, mean-minded man into thinking that the sad, beautiful lady of the house has fallen in love with him. He is reading what he thinks is a love letter to him from the lady. He says:

. . . for every reason excites to this, that my lady loves
me . . . I thank my stars, I am happy.

Twelfth Night / 2.5 / Lines 160, 165

But the letter's a forgery, written by the bunch of crazy people now watching him while he reads. What will happen next time the stuffy man meets the lady?

There are lots more amazing rooms, and if you go into them you will find trial scenes, battles, love potions, cruel kings, civil wars, assassinations, riots, witches, fairies, jesters, even a statue that comes to life. You will also meet people with deep and powerful emotions — wild jealousy, crazed hunger for power, terrible sadness, great happiness, sneering contempt.

All this may sound extraordinary, but Shakespeare lived in extraordinary times.

Extraordinary and Dangerous Times

So what was it like in England when Shakespeare was writing? These were dangerous times— even for a writer! A few years earlier, one of the most famous playwrights of the day, Christopher Marlowe, had been stabbed to death during a fight in a tavern. Another playwright, Ben Jonson, had killed someone and managed to get off with nothing more than having his left thumb branded with a T for Tyburn—the place where he'd be executed if he was caught again.

And, strange as it may seem, these were especially dangerous times if you were the king or queen. Shakespeare lived under two monarchs: Elizabeth I and James I. Elizabeth was imprisoned in the Tower of London by her half sister. Her father, Henry VIII, had her mother beheaded, and Elizabeth herself ordered the execution of her cousin, Mary, Queen of Scots. When James was king, Guy Fawkes and his friends tried to blow him up in the Houses of Parliament.

Shakespeare lived at a time when ordinary people didn't choose who ruled over them. Countries were ruled by someone who claimed that he (or, very rarely, she) had a right to rule because he belonged to a particular family. This family would say there was a "royal line" that went back and back and that proved that they were the "true" rulers. Many ordinary people looked up to these monarchs as if they were almost gods.

But in Britain several families claimed that they were the "true" rulers, and you have to remember that such families were rich

enough to raise armies against each other. This meant that civil war—war between people in the same country—was always possible. Every year brought news of plots and rebellions. There was also a big war with Spain. There were bloody battles in Ireland and Holland.

Shakespeare wrote plays about the powerful families—the lords and dukes and princes—who wanted to rule England. In these plays, and in others set in ancient Rome, we watch exciting scenes of civil wars, battles, rebellions, poor people's riots, conspiracies, and wars between countries. And while all this is going on, the characters often discuss what makes a good ruler. What if your ruler were no good? Would it be right to get rid of that ruler and put someone else in his or her place? Who should decide that? Should that be an argument left to the great families that had always ruled?

Some of the people who thought they should have a say were people with money and power but no "royal line." It was only thirty-three years after Shakespeare died that such people had the king's head chopped off and then chose Oliver Cromwell—a ruler with no royal line who didn't even call himself a king!

Shakespeare lived in extraordinary and dangerous times.

In Shakespeare's time religion was much more important in everyone's lives than it is today. Nearly all British people described themselves as Christian but where there had once been only one Christian Church, there were now many. And wherever one kind of Christian gained power, they nearly always ended up trying to imprison or kill off the other kinds. All over Europe people were fighting huge bloody battles and civil wars against each other.

In England the trouble involved the ruling family, the Tudors. When the Tudor monarch was a Roman Catholic, Protestants were persecuted, arrested, and sometimes burned at the stake. And when Elizabeth—a Protestant—came to the throne, it was extremely dangerous to be a Roman Catholic. Elizabeth had 123 Catholic priests executed.

Protestants also fought each other. Some, nicknamed "Puritans" and "Quakers," were inventing a whole new way of life and preaching an end to high living, fun and games, gambling, sports, drinking, overeating, and street festivals. Shakespeare came across these people not only as refugees from Holland but also as the new rulers of the City of London, with the power to close theatres and ban plays. Small wonder we catch a glimpse of one or two unpleasant Puritans in his plays!

In some parts of Europe, Roman Catholics were in power; in others, Protestants. So the discussions over who should be king and what makes a good ruler were intertwined in Shakespeare's lifetime with questions about the right way to be a Christian.

Shakespeare lived among all this political and religious talk. But it wasn't all talk. There was a lot of plotting and spying and murder going on as well. You often find people in his plays talking about the making and breaking of kings, as well as treachery and treason:

Peace, impudent and shameless Warwick, peace!
Proud setter-up and puller-down of kings!

Henry VI Part 3 / 3.3 / Lines 156–7

Shakespeare would have known that if you backed the wrong man, you could end up stabbed to death or executed. What's more, with the streets full of soldiers and ex-soldiers, there was always someone around who knew a lot about killing:

. . . when the searching eye of heaven is hid
Behind the globe, that lights the lower world,
Then thieves and robbers range abroad unseen
In murders and in outrage bloody here . . .

Richard II / 3.2 / Lines 33–6

But these dangerous times were also times of great change. Explorers were heading off all around the globe, discovering, among other things, that the earth was round and not flat. The people of England and Europe now knew that there were many different countries in the world, and that vast amounts of money could be made if you came back to England with valuable cargoes. Just after Shakespeare was born, John Hawkins found another way to make money: taking people from West Africa across the Atlantic Ocean to sell in the Caribbean as slaves. In one of Shakespeare's plays we see a slave arguing for the right to live on his own land:

This island's mine, by Sycorax my mother,
Which thou tak'st from me. When thou cam'st first,
Thou strok'st me and made much of me, wouldst give me
Water with berries in't . . .

The Tempest / 1.2 / Lines 333–6

And he goes on to complain:

. . . and here you sty me
In this hard rock, whiles you do keep from me
The rest o'th' island.

The Tempest / 1.2 / Lines 344–6

We also see Shakespeare's characters realizing just how powerful money is. Two daughters turn against their own father because of their greed; a rich merchant nearly loses his life when he loses his money; and a nobleman despairs when he sees what evil things people will do for gold. He calls gold a "yellow slave":

This yellow slave
Will knit and break religions . . .

Timon of Athens / 4.3 / Lines 34–5

and goes on to say how it will turn thieves into lords and then politicians will approve of them.

Some other people in Shakespeare's time were discovering extraordinary things by investigating plants and animals, studying languages, reading old books from ancient Greece and Rome, and reading new books from Italy and France.

This desire to explore and discover was made easier by a revolution in how people communicated with each other. In England and Wales a hundred years earlier, most of the people who could read and write worked in the Church. Now, more and more people were getting an education. Many could read, even if they couldn't write. Jokes, stories, poetry, plays, and ideas about politics were all appearing in print. You could find them written down in pamphlets, sometimes on single sheets of paper sold by ballad sellers, and, of course, in books.

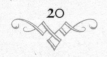

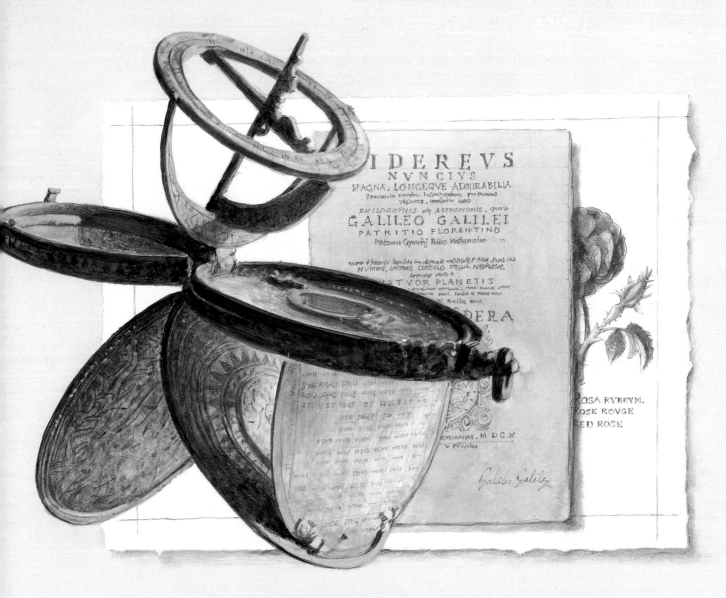

All this meant that knowledge was no longer something that you had to remember. It was something you could store on a page in a book in your pocket or in your house. And now reading was not just for priests, bishops, and the people close to the king. Someone like Shakespeare, from a tradesman's family living in a country town, could turn the knowledge he found in books into lines, scenes, and whole plays. And what's more, he was not just an Englishman writing about things in England, but someone who took books, plays, poems, and folktales from Italy, ancient Rome, and Arab countries, and turned them into dramas.

By the time Shakespeare was thirteen, his father's business was going downhill. It is only guesswork, but he may have had to leave school at this time because his father could not pay for him to stay there. Some people think that Shakespeare became a butcher's boy! This is because in his plays he seems to know so much about the trade of butchering meat. Others think he may have started training or done time as a lawyer, a doctor, a sailor, a falconer, or a gardener because the plays seem to show so much knowledge of these professions too. Of course, he may just have worked in his father's business, making and selling leather goods.

But let's face it, we don't really know very much about how Shakespeare spent his childhood and teenage years. We know what he *might* have thought about growing up, though, from the words of an old shepherd in one of his plays:

I would there were no age between ten and
three-and-twenty, or that youth would sleep out the rest;
for there is nothing in the between but getting wenches
with child, wronging the ancientry, stealing, fighting . . .

The Winter's Tale / 3.3 / Lines 58–62

in other words, teenage pregnancy, being rude to old people, and stealing and fighting. What's new? Shakespeare himself was a teenage father, and we don't catch another glimpse of him till he's twenty-eight years old and living in London.

ANOTHER WAY TO FIND OUT SOMETHING ABOUT SHAKESPEARE
IS TO LOOK AT THE CITY WHERE HE SPENT SO MUCH
OF HIS LIFE:

LONDON

GREATER LONDON today has almost ten million people living in it. In Shakespeare's time only two hundred thousand people lived there. Most of them had been born in England and Scotland but about five thousand had come from other countries; many were Puritan refugees as there were religious wars going on in and around Holland.

Even though Tudor London might seem small by today's standards, it was seen in its time to be a huge, bustling, important place, ". . . too much pestered with people" as the historian John Stow wrote, with many living in "multitudes of base tenements."

Right through the middle of the city ran the River Thames. It was packed with boats, and its three miles of quayside were busy with people loading and unloading goods from all over Britain, Europe, and newly explored parts of the world. "Most of the inhabitants are employed in buying and selling merchandise, and trading in almost every corner of the world," said the Duke of Wurtemberg who was visiting London in 1592. All walks of life could be found in London. There was the court with its various palaces, where Queen Elizabeth I and then King James I lived, surrounded by hundreds of advisers, servants, entertainers, and hangers-on.

There were the very rich who were setting up new banking and money-lending businesses. Such people might have owned two houses—a big country house just outside London and a grand townhouse.

There were the merchants who got together in groups called liveries and through their line of business—wool, gold, manufacturing, or whatever—had a big say in how London and England were run. There were thousands of tradesmen and shopkeepers living and working in small buildings or on stalls in the markets. There were the people who worked for all these others—the laborers and journeymen, as they were often called. And there were the out-of-work poor—the unemployed soldiers, old people, beggars, and street people. In and among them all, thousands of people such as bishops, priests, nuns, and friars lived and worked in the Church.

Shakespeare's London.

In Shakespeare's plays, we meet the people of London. Within sight of the whole city stood the Tower, a place of dreadful executions and plots, and in *Hamlet* we find a prince walking the battlements of a castle full of murder and rumors of murder:

My father's spirit in arms! All is not well.
I doubt some foul play. Would the night were come.
Till then, sit still, my soul. Foul deeds will rise,
Though all the earth o'erwhelm them, to men's eyes.

Hamlet / 1.2 / Lines 254–7

In *The Merchant of Venice* Antonio, a rich merchant, wheels and deals with a moneylender:

Thou know'st that all my fortunes are at sea,
Neither have I money nor commodity {*commodity = valuable goods*}
To raise a present sum. {*present sum = a sum of ready money*}

The Merchant of Venice / 1.1 / Lines 177–9

In *Henry IV Part 2* a gang of ruffians is called up to fight in the army. In *Romeo and Juliet* Juliet rushes to a friar to find a way to marry her lover in secret. In *The Winter's Tale* Autolycus sells ballads and stories. And in *Coriolanus* people riot over high prices, just as they did in London in Shakespeare's time.

We meet gravediggers, lawyers, schoolteachers, servants, and many, many more. We hear from people who want to kill their king, and we meet angry crowds of poor people. Like London itself, Shakespeare's plays teem with life.

AS YOU LOOK ACROSS THE CENTURIES, THE KINDS
OF ENTERTAINMENT THAT PEOPLE ENJOY CHANGE.

THEATRE IN THE MAKING

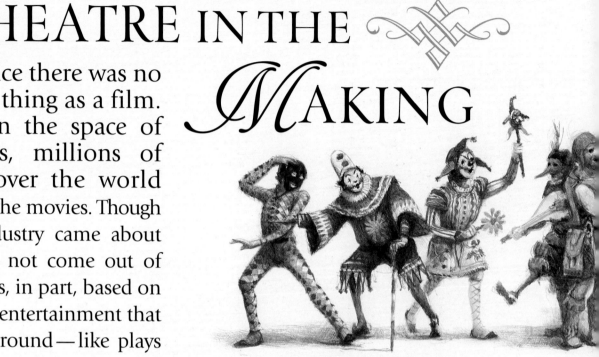

Once there was no such thing as a film. Then in the space of a few years, millions of people all over the world were going to the movies. Though the movie industry came about quickly, it did not come out of nowhere: it was, in part, based on other kinds of entertainment that were already around—like plays and music hall shows.

It was a bit like that with the Elizabethan theatre Shakespeare found himself working in. When he was a boy, nearly everyone would have known about two kinds of popular shows.

Mummers' plays were put on by local people at festival times and tell the story of St. George, who is killed and then magically rises up, usually cured by a crazy doctor. The characters speak in rhymes, sing songs, and tell a few local jokes. These plays could be put on anywhere—in town squares, barns, or fields. There are parts of Britain where they're still performed, sometimes in schools, and there's a special pleasure in thinking that Shakespeare, living as he did in the countryside, would certainly have known about Mummers' plays.

The other kind of popular show was the Mystery play—sometimes called the Miracle play. Nowadays we all know about the Nativity play, written and rewritten by ordinary people and acted out by anyone of any age.

In Shakespeare's time, people used to write and act out many more of the stories from the Bible. In some of these we find invented scenes, like an argument between Noah and his wife, or a man who steals a sheep from one of the shepherds in the Nativity play. Shakespeare is probably mentioning these Mystery plays when Hamlet talks of an actor who overacts as one who **out-Herods Herod**, that infamous king of Palestine when Jesus was born.

People also acted out versions of old plays and stories that weren't from the Bible—we see this in *A Midsummer Night's Dream* when a group of workmen stage a play called *Pyramus and Thisbe* about two lovers who die.

Another kind of play—the Morality play—started appearing about a hundred years before Shakespeare's birth. This was a religious entertainment in which the characters had names like Charity and Folly and argued amongst themselves about the best way to behave.

As well as all these different kinds of theatre, nearly everyone would at some time in their lives have seen big public pageants and processions, rather like the ones we see today, with dances and mimes enacted and re-enacted as part of the procession. Kings, queens, dukes, and lords were fond of all these entertainments, which they put on in public or in their palaces and mansions. They also enjoyed shows called "masques"—a kind of fancy dress dance, often with songs and a magical theme. We come across them in Shakespeare's plays, and we know that

Queen Elizabeth's father, Henry VIII, took part in an Italian-style masque, dressed up in gold garments. He and the other masquers were hidden under "visors and caps of gold," and after the banquet was done, they "came in . . . and desired the ladies to dance." There is every chance young Shakespeare would have seen a variety of entertainments: a royal procession, local pageants, and plays put on by touring players. We know that in his youth, visiting players came twenty-five times to Stratford and that Elizabeth I visited a nearby castle where a great pageant with water displays was put on for her.

Shakespeare's childhood and youth mark a time in England when teams of traveling players toured the country putting on shows. Sometimes they had a rich person to support them, and then they were called things like Lord Strange's Men or the Lord Chamberlain's Men. Shakespeare himself joined a group of players, first as an actor and then as a resident playwright. It was these traveling players who made it possible for the huge revolution in playwriting and theatre that took place in Shakespeare's time.

Traveling players performing in the courtyard of an inn.

Theatre was becoming more popular and more groups of traveling players were getting together. They all needed plays to act in and places to perform them. When these groups started out, they had no theatres. Sometimes they put on shows for the rich in big rooms and halls around the country. But when they performed in the courtyards of inns, they reached a much wider audience. We know that inns in London were being used for plays from just before Shakespeare's birth, and by the time he came to London and joined the Lord Chamberlain's Men, the first theatres had just been built. It was a good time to be in "show biz." For the first time, actors were making enough money to build and own theatres.

And something else was happening. Some of the cleverest minds alive were writing plays full of action, tension, and full-fledged character. Young Christopher Marlowe wrote a play called *Tamburlaine the Great* about an incredibly violent king. Clever people with an education, like Ben Jonson, were writing plays full of wit and learning. It was just like the birth of the film industry or TV: new companies, a new way of putting on shows, and a desperate need for new scripts.

Throughout Shakespeare's life, new playwrights were appearing, hundreds of new plays were being written, and theatres were popping up all around the edges of the City of London.

THE NEW THEATRES

THESE THEATRES HAD A SPECIAL SHAPE. IF YOU GO TO THE GLOBE THEATRE IN LONDON OR TO OTHER SIMILAR THEATRES IN THE U.S.A., CANADA, JAPAN, AND NEW ZEALAND, YOU CAN SEE WHAT THEY LOOKED LIKE. The buildings were round or octagonal with an open-air space in the middle and covered galleries around the edges. The stage was at one side and stuck out into the audience. When Juliet

appears at her window, dreaming of Romeo, she would have been on a balcony above the stage, while the ghost in *Macbeth* would probably have come up through a trap door in the floor. There were no curtains across the front of the stage, so the beginnings and ends of scenes were just marked by the actors coming on and off. There were no elaborate stage paintings or sets either, and that's why, over and over again, we hear the characters in Shakespeare's plays saying where they are and what they can see:

But look, the morn in russet mantle clad {*russet mantle = red coat*}
Walks o'er the dew of yon high eastern hill. {*o'er = over*} {*yon = that*}

Hamlet / 1.1 / Lines 147–8

48

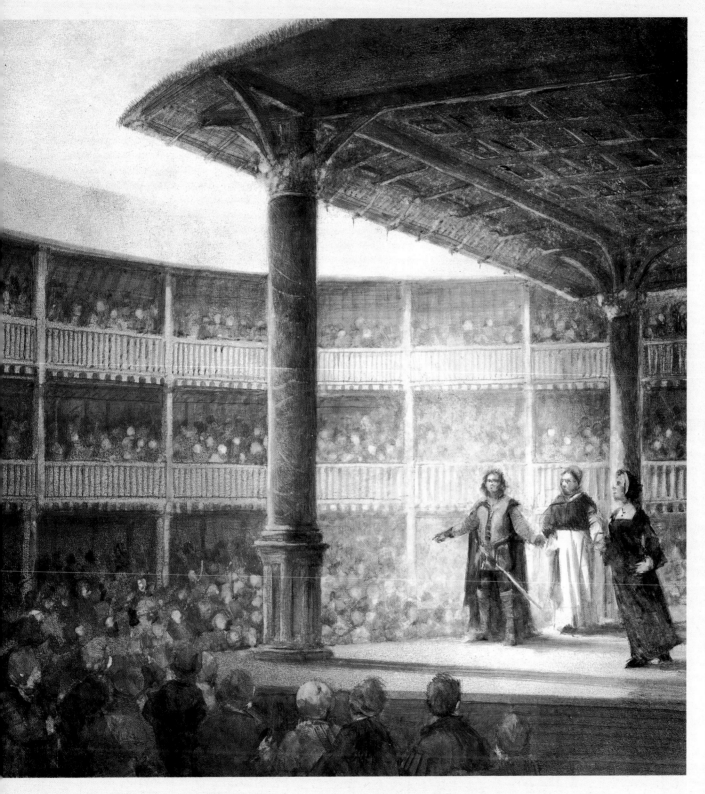

A performance at the Globe Theatre.

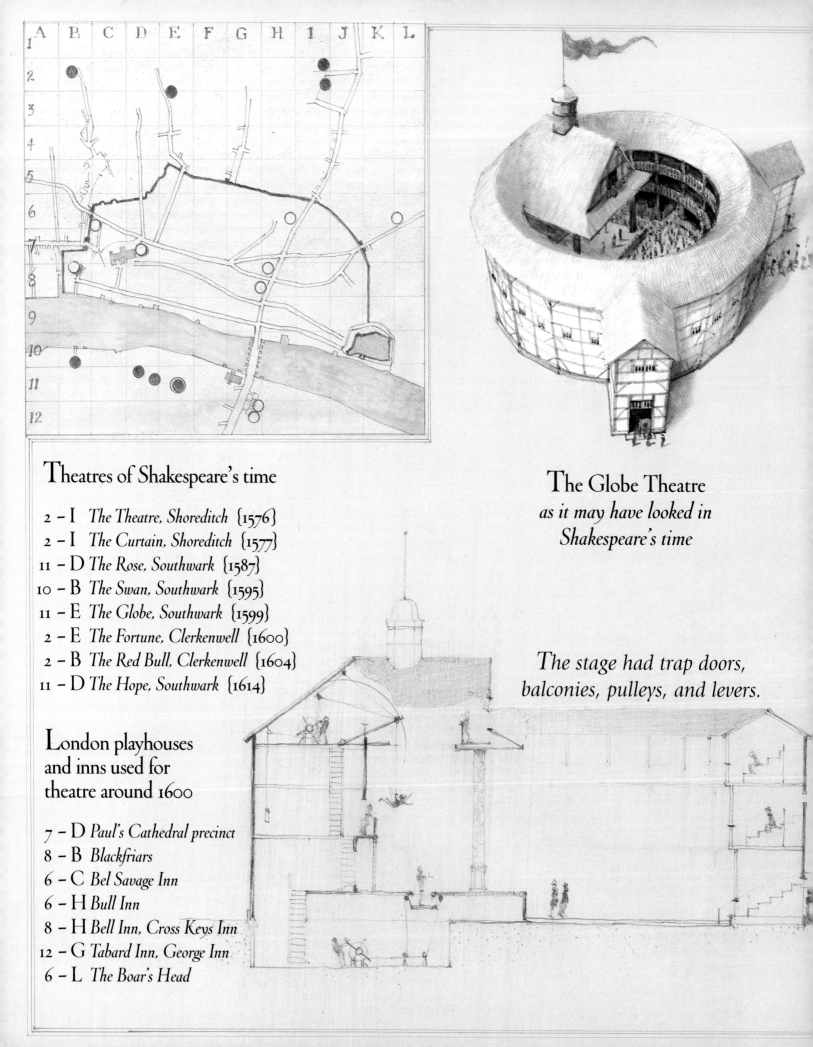

Theatres of Shakespeare's time

2 – I *The Theatre, Shoreditch* {1576}
2 – I *The Curtain, Shoreditch* {1577}
11 – D *The Rose, Southwark* {1587}
10 – B *The Swan, Southwark* {1595}
11 – E *The Globe, Southwark* {1599}
2 – E *The Fortune, Clerkenwell* {1600}
2 – B *The Red Bull, Clerkenwell* {1604}
11 – D *The Hope, Southwark* {1614}

London playhouses and inns used for theatre around 1600

7 – D *Paul's Cathedral precinct*
8 – B *Blackfriars*
6 – C *Bel Savage Inn*
6 – H *Bull Inn*
8 – H *Bell Inn, Cross Keys Inn*
12 – G *Tabard Inn, George Inn*
6 – L *The Boar's Head*

The Globe Theatre
as it may have looked in Shakespeare's time

The stage had trap doors, balconies, pulleys, and levers.

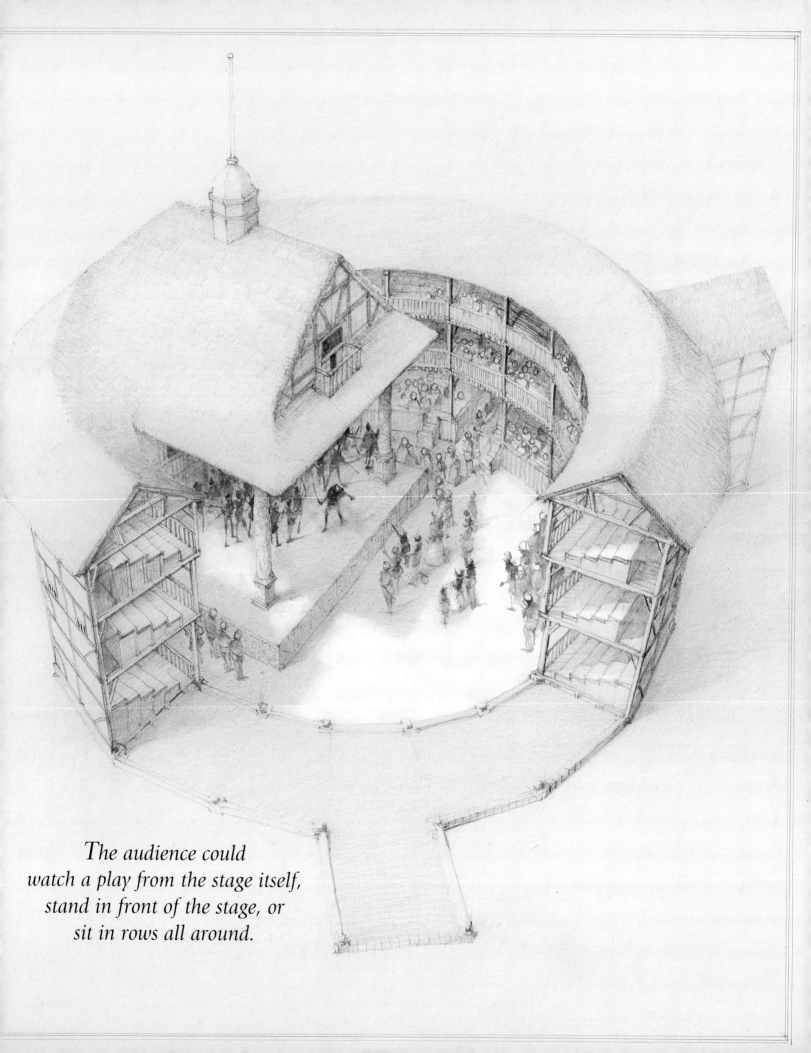

The audience could
watch a play from the stage itself,
stand in front of the stage, or
sit in rows all around.

In the introductions and end pieces to his plays Shakespeare often asks the audience to think about the imagination that's needed to enjoy a play:

Think, when we talk of horses, that you see them,
Printing their proud hoofs i' th' receiving earth . . .

Henry V / Prologue / Lines 26–7

Because there were no theatre lights, the characters often have to say what time of day it is:

How sweet the moonlight sleeps upon this bank!

The Merchant of Venice / 5.1 / Line 54

No women ever acted in plays, so their parts were taken by boys. This may be why we find such vivid descriptions of women:

O, she doth teach the torches to burn bright!
It seems she hangs upon the cheek of night
As a rich jewel in an Ethiope's ear—
Beauty too rich for use, for earth too dear.

Romeo and Juliet / 1.5 / Lines 43–6

Some of the audience watched the play from the stage itself, and some stood in front of the stage looking up at it, while the rest sat in rows all aound. A Swiss visitor called Thomas Platter described these audiences in 1599:

. . . anyone who remains on the level standing pays only one English penny: but if he wants to sit, he is let in at a further door, and there he gives another penny. If he desires to sit on a cushion in the most comfortable place of all, where he not only sees everything well, but can also be seen, then he gives yet another English penny at another door.

While the plays were on, some people talked, shouted, ate, drank, and heckled. One of Shakespeare's characters says:

**These are the youths that thunder at a playhouse,
and fight for bitten apples . . .**

Henry VIII / 5.3 / Lines 58–9

The Puritans in their churches and in their council chambers weren't happy. They didn't like the way plays led to "frays and quarrels" and tried to ban them:

**Satan hath not a more speedy way, fitter school to work
and teach his desire to bring men and women into his
snare of concupiscence and filthy lusts of whoredom,
than those places and plays . . .**

This is a way of saying that theatres tempted people into all kinds of sin: overeating, drunkenness, and the wrong kind of sex.

The Puritans kept trying to close the theatres, and they had to be closed again and again because of the plague, which killed over a fifth of the population of London at the time. But though it wasn't always easy to put on plays, nothing could stop the growing popularity of the theatre. By 1604, Shakespeare and his company were well on the way to becoming national celebrities.

APART FROM POEMS AND PLAYS, WE KNOW OF ONE OTHER THING THAT SHAKESPEARE WROTE: HIS WILL. PEOPLE HAVE PORED OVER IT FOR CENTURIES, TRYING TO FIGURE OUT WHAT HE REALLY MEANT.

THE *Will*

The phrase that amuses many people is where he says that he will leave his wife his "second best bed." Why didn't he leave her his best bed? they ask. Perhaps he didn't love her. Perhaps she knew that she was going to get the best bed, but he was simply saying she could have the second best as well.

In the name of God Amen

... my last will and Testament ...

NON SANZ DROICT

Historians have argued over these words. Some say that his wife would have got one-third of all Shakespeare's Stratford houses and lands anyway—the "widow's dower." Not so, say recent historians. In that part of the country, widows didn't have this right. So maybe Shakespeare's wife did only get his second-best bed and had to rely on the goodwill of her family and friends to support her for the rest of her life.

Whatever the truth is, we can definitely say that, in his will, Shakespeare left more of what he owned to one daughter, Susanna, than to the other, Judith. Susanna could read and was married to a doctor, while Judith couldn't read and had just married someone who was known in Stratford to be a rather shady, dishonest fellow. What's more, Shakespeare rewrote his will to make sure that his property and wealth would go on being passed down through Susanna's children. When you match this up with the fact that he had helped create a coat of arms for his family, you build up a picture of someone who was very interested in starting a new, well-off family line—what's known as a dynasty.

We don't know whether any character in a Shakespeare play is saying something that Shakespeare thought about his own life, but in *King Lear* he shows us an old man struggling with how to share his wealth among his children. Perhaps, and we can only ever say "perhaps," Shakespeare spent some time in his life worrying about who to leave his money to. Perhaps, like King Lear, he also worried about whether leaving more money to one child than another meant loving one child more than another. When King Lear finally comes to see that Cordelia, the daughter he rejected, really loved him, he has been driven mad, but in his madness he has a vision and he says to her:

Come, let's away to prison.
We two alone will sing like birds i'th' cage.
When thou dost ask me blessing, I'll kneel down
And ask of thee forgiveness; so we'll live,
And pray, and sing, and tell old tales, and laugh
At gilded butterflies . . .

King Lear / 5.3 / Lines 8–13

When all is said, we know next to nothing about what made Shakespeare happy, angry, or sad. In other words, we don't know anything about his emotional life. But through the documents that have survived, we do have a very clear picture of someone who started out as the son of a small tradesman and ended as a wealthy landowner. He was also, of course, the most famous writer of his time.

Shakespeare died on April 23, 1616, around his fifty-second birthday. On his tomb is written:

Good friend, for Jesu's sake forbear
To dig the dust enclosed here.
Blest be the man that spares these stones
And cursed be he that moves my bones.

Why there is such a threat, no one knows.

DO YOU EVER SAY THAT SOMEONE IS **TONGUE-TIED** OR THAT SOMETHING IS **AS DULL AS DISHWATER**? HAVE YOU EVER SAID THAT SOMEONE WOULDN'T **BUDGE AN INCH**? HAVE YOU EVER HEARD SOMEONE SAY THAT HE OR SHE HAS **SEEN BETTER DAYS**? PERHAPS YOU'VE HEARD PEOPLE SAY HE'S HIS **OWN FLESH AND BLOOD**, IT **SET YOUR TEETH ON EDGE**, THAT **THE GAME IS UP**, IT'S **WITHOUT RHYME OR REASON**, IT HAPPENED IN **ONE FELL SWOOP**, IT **MELTED INTO THIN AIR**, **THAT'S THE LONG AND SHORT OF IT**, AND **THE TRUTH WILL OUT**.

THE LEGACY

If you've used or heard any of these expressions, that was Shakespeare talking. Some words we use every day first appeared in his writing and were perhaps invented by him: *hint, leapfrog, lonely, excellent,* and *gloomy* are just some of them.

But it's not only words and expressions that have lasted. Every day of every year someone somewhere in the world is reading Shakespeare, and people are acting in his plays and watching them. Somewhere, someone like me is writing a book about his writing.

**Tomorrow,
and
tomorrow,
and
tomorrow**
Macbeth

**My salad days,
When I was
green in
judgement,
cold in blood**
Antony and Cleopatra

**If music be
the food
of love,
play on**
Twelfth Night

Fear no more
the heat
o'th' sun
Cymbeline

We are such stuff
As dreams are
made on
The Tempest

Friends, Romans,
countrymen,
lend me your ears.
Julius Caesar

**Once more
unto the breach,
dear friends**
Henry V

**To be,
or not to be;
that is
the question**
Hamlet

**Blow, winds, and
crack your cheeks!**
King Lear

O Romeo, Romeo,
wherefore art
thou Romeo?
Romeo and Juliet

Let us sit upon
the ground,
And tell sad stories
of the death of kings
Richard II

The course of true love
never did run smooth
A Midsummer Night's Dream

The quality of mercy
is not strained.
The Merchant of Venice

What all this means is that Shakespeare's writing is part of world culture. His words are so familiar that, when people try to understand something, or imagine something, or describe it, their minds turn to a scene or character from Shakespeare.

Everyone comes to Shakespeare's writing for different reasons and takes different things from it. When people are feeling tired or fed up they sometimes think of the murderous king Macbeth, in despair of his life, seeing the passage of time as a terrible burden:

Tomorrow, and tomorrow, and tomorrow
Creeps in this petty pace from day to day
To the last syllable of recorded time . . .

Macbeth / 5.5 / Lines 18–20

Some people enjoy Shakespeare's colorful insults: **Pernicious blood-sucker of sleeping men . . . long-tongued, babbling gossip . . . smiling, smooth, detested parasites . . . loathsomest scab in Greece.**

Some people like using little phrases from Shakespeare as a way of answering or interrupting. They might say: **But me no buts** when they want someone to stop giving excuses; **Parting is such sweet sorrow** when saying goodbye; **Why, this is very midsummer madness** when crazy things are going on; **The lady protests too much, methinks** when they suspect someone who's overreacting is probably guilty; **All that glisters is not gold** to mean something may not be as good as it looks.

Sometimes it's the jokes people remember. In *Twelfth Night*, for instance, a noblewoman calls to her servants to get rid of the jester: **Take the fool away**, and the jester comes in with, **Do you not hear, fellows? Take away the lady**. And in *Much Ado About Nothing*

Shakespeare pokes fun at the way an ordinary policeman gets all mixed up when he tries to use posh legal language. He says:

Our watch, sir, have indeed comprehended   {watch = police}
two auspicious persons . . .

Much Ado About Nothing / 3.5 / Lines 43–4

instead of "apprehended two suspicious persons." Later, he says:

Marry, sir, they have committed false report, moreover they have spoken untruths, secondarily they are slanders, sixth and lastly they have belied a lady, thirdly they have verified unjust things, and to conclude, they are lying knaves.

Much Ado About Nothing / 5.1 / Lines 208–12

So the policeman ends up saying the same thing in six different ways. Not that he can count either!

For more than three hundred years after Shakespeare's death, we find that people didn't always perform the whole of his plays and that sometimes they rewrote them. There was even a time when actors used to put shows together of what they thought were the great speeches.

In the last hundred years there have been other changes. The plays have been put on in modern dress as operas, musicals, ballets, and films. For some of these performances the original scripts were cut or changed. Perhaps the most famous and striking has been *Romeo and Juliet* starring Leonardo DiCaprio and Claire Danes. Using the words of Shakespeare's play, but cut down by well over two-thirds, the film is set in modern America, backed by rock music. Some people thought that it wrecked Shakespeare but others thought it was one of the best ways ever to keep Shakespeare alive.

If any part of this book has grabbed your attention, if there's anything about Shakespeare and what he wrote that has made you stop and wonder, then don't leave it at that. You could rent a video of a Shakespeare film. Perhaps a theatre near you is putting on one of the plays. Why not go? But before you do, you could find one of those books that tell the story of the play. If you read it before you go, it might help you to concentrate. If you're studying Shakespeare at school, it's great to get a chance to act out some of it—even just one short scene. Then you see that Shakespeare didn't really write books, he wrote scripts—scenes and speeches for people to say out loud and act out in front of other people.

Shakespeare himself knew just how powerful this can be. In *Hamlet* Prince Hamlet arranges for a group of traveling players to put on a play that acts out the murder of his father. The players perform it in front of Claudius, the new king, the man who actually committed the murder. At the moment when the play shows a man poisoning a king, just as Claudius has murdered Hamlet's father, the real Claudius can't bear it any longer and rushes out shouting: **Give me some light.**

Yes, watching a play—watching a Shakespeare play—can be that striking. Try it. ᘏᘏᘏ

Give me some light.

Shakespeare's age appears after the date. The dates for his plays are what scholars suggest. They are not certain or definite.

1557
~ England begins a two-year war with France.

1558
~ Elizabeth, daughter of Henry VIII and Anne Boleyn, becomes Queen of England.

~ Explorer Anthony Jenkinson travels around Russia.

1560
~ The Geneva Bible — an early version of the Bible in English — is published.

1561
~ The first play to be written in the same rhythm as Shakespeare's plays — blank verse — is performed in London (*Gorboduc* by T. Norton and T. Sackville).

1562
~ John Hawkins is the first Englishman to trade slaves, taking them from Sierra Leone in Africa to Hispaniola (now Cuba) in the Caribbean.

1563
~ Twenty thousand people die of the plague in London.

1564
◆**William Shakespeare is born in Henley Street, Stratford-upon-Avon, son of John and Mary, on or around April 23.**
~ Two hundred people die of the plague in Stratford.
~ Work starts on Britain's first canal.

1567
Three years old.
~ London's first specially built theatre is made at the Red Lion, Whitechapel.
~ James Stuart is crowned James VI of Scotland at one year old.

1568
Four years old.
~ The Geneva Bible is revised and published as the Bishops' Bible. Shakespeare would have read both versions.

1569
Five years old.
~ Elizabeth I crushes the Revolt of the Northern Earls, a Roman Catholic uprising in the north of England.

1570
Six years old.
◆**Shakespeare's father is found guilty of usury — making too much profit from lending money.**
~ Pope Pius V excommunicates Elizabeth I — which means she is forbidden to be part of the Roman Catholic Church.

1571
Seven years old.
~ The Ridolfi Plot against the Queen.
~ A law is passed saying that a person found doing something under instruction from the Pope will be charged with treason and, if found guilty, will be executed.

1576
Twelve years old.
◆**John Shakespeare, William's father, is almost completely broke.**
~ Traveling players — Leicester's Men and Worcester's Men — visit Stratford.
~ The Theatre, a theatre that William Shakespeare will use, opens in Shoreditch, London.

The Theatre

~ Vagrants (unemployed people on the move) are forced to go to Bridewell, a kind of prison.
~ Explorer Martin Frobisher travels in what is now northern Canada.

1577
Thirteen years old.
~ The Curtain Theatre opens in Shoreditch.
~ Francis Drake leaves Plymouth to sail around the world.

1579
Fifteen years old.
~ Traveling players — Lord Strange's Men and the Countess of Essex's Men — visit Stratford.
~ *The School of Abuse*, a pamphlet attacking plays and poetry, is published.
~ A rebellion in Ireland is ruthlessly put down by English troops.
~ Francis Drake lands just north of what is now San Francisco and names it New Albion, part of England.

1580
Sixteen years old.
~ Nine Roman Catholics land in Dover with the aim of over-throwing the Queen. The Roman Catholic Church has promised the assassination of Queen Elizabeth would be "a glorious work" and not a sin.

1581
Seventeen years old.
~ To convert to being a Roman Catholic is now treason in England. A person can be sentenced to death for it.

1582
Eighteen years old.
◆**Shakespeare marries Anne Hathaway.**

1583

Nineteen years old.

◆Susanna, William and Anne's first child, is baptized.

～ *The Anatomy of Abuses*, a pamphlet attacking plays and players, is published.

～ The Throckmorton Plot to kill the Queen. The Spanish ambassador is involved.

～ Explorer Humphrey Gilbert starts a settlement in Newfoundland, now in Canada.

1585

Twenty-one years old.

◆Hamnet and Judith, William and Anne's twins, are baptized.

～ A member of Parliament is executed for threatening to kill the Queen.

～ England is at war with Spain, and English troops are sent to Holland.

1586

Twenty-two years old.

～ The Babington Plot against Elizabeth. Her cousin Mary, Queen of Scots, is accused of being part of it.

～ As a way of trying to control Puritans, a law is passed saying that all pamphlets on religion must be approved by the Church.

～ The first potatoes are brought to Britain from Colombia.

1587

Twenty-three years old.

◆Shakespeare probably arrives in London around this time.

～ The Rose Theatre opens on Bankside, Southwark, London, near the present Globe Theatre.

～ Christopher Marlowe's spectacular play *Tamburlaine the Great* and Thomas Kyd's *The Spanish Tragedy* are written around this time.

～ Elizabeth I orders the execution of her cousin Mary, Queen of Scots, for being involved with the Babington Plot.

～ A member of Parliament, Peter Wentworth, is imprisoned for asking for more freedom of speech.

1588

Twenty-four years old.

～ New plays and productions in London's theatres start to happen from now on.

～ A Catholic priest is executed in public close to the Theatre.

～ The Spanish Armada is defeated off the coast of England.

{ 1589–91 }

SHAKESPEARE
WRITES
★HENRY VI
(IN THREE PARTS)

1591

Twenty-seven years old.

～ The Queen's favorite, the Earl of Essex, is in France helping Protestants to fight Roman Catholics.

～ Explorer James Lancaster leaves for the East Indies (now Indonesia).

1592

Twenty-eight years old.

◆Shakespeare's play *Henry VI* is performed at the Rose Theatre.

～ Robert Greene writes his attack on Shakespeare, calling him an "upstart crow" (see page 25).

～ London theatres are officially closed due to labor riots by apprentices.

～ London clothing workers in Southwark (near where the Globe Theatre will be) riot against changes in the industry and the arrival of foreign workers from France and Holland.

～ A midsummer street festival near Bankside ends in bloodshed as the authorities kill "several innocent persons."

～ Severe plague in London for two years. The theatres are closed.

～ Spanish treasure is seized by English ships.

{ 1592–3 }

SHAKESPEARE
WRITES
★RICHARD III
★TITUS
ANDRONICUS
★VENUS
AND ADONIS

1593

Twenty-nine years old.

◆Shakespeare's long poem *Venus and Adonis* is entered in the Stationers' Register. This gives a bookseller the license to print and publish it as a book.

～ Playwright Christopher Marlowe is stabbed to death in a tavern brawl.

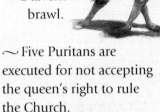

～ Five Puritans are executed for not accepting the queen's right to rule the Church.

～ Eleven thousand people die of the plague in London.

{ 1593–4 }

SHAKESPEARE
WRITES
★THE COMEDY
OF ERRORS
★THE TAMING
OF THE SHREW
★THE RAPE
OF LUCRECE

1594

Thirty years old.

◆*The Comedy of Errors* is performed at Gray's Inn in London.

◆Shakespeare's long poem *The Rape of Lucrece* is entered in the Stationers' Register.

◆Shakespeare is listed as one of the Lord Chamberlain's Men.

~ Bad harvests in England bring high prices and starvation.

~ The Queen's doctor, a Portuguese Jew, is accused of trying to poison her and is executed.

~ English troops are sent to put down an uprising by Roman Catholics in Ireland.

{ 1594–5 }

SHAKESPEARE WRITES
★THE TWO GENTLEMEN OF VERONA
★LOVE'S LABOUR'S LOST

1595

Thirty-one years old.

~ Theatres in London are officially closed for two months after riots over food prices.

~ London authorities claim that "disorderly people of the common sort . . . assemble themselves" and do "un-godly" things at holiday time, and "apprentices and servants" catch plague from the new playhouses.

~ Famous Roman Catholic priest and poet Robert Southwell is tortured and executed for treason.

~ Spain raids Cornish seaside towns of Penzance and Mousehole.

~ England is at war with Ireland.

~ Explorer Sir Walter Raleigh is in the north-east part of Latin America, what is now Venezuela.

{ 1595–6 }

SHAKESPEARE WRITES
★ROMEO AND JULIET
★RICHARD II
★A MIDSUMMER NIGHT'S DREAM

1596

Thirty-two years old.

◆Shakespeare's eleven-year-old son, Hamnet, dies.

~ There are riots and rebellions in Oxfordshire and the Midlands against "gentlemen," enclosures, poverty, and hunger.

~ A message to the Queen's adviser warns that this year "will be the hardest year for the poor in man's memory" and that as a result "there would be cutting of throats."

~ The first water-flushing toilet is installed in the Queen's palace in Richmond.

{ 1596–7 }

SHAKESPEARE WRITES
★KING JOHN
★THE MERCHANT OF VENICE

1597

Thirty-three years old.

◆Shakespeare buys New Place, a house in Stratford.

◆Shakespeare is reported for not paying taxes in St. Helen's parish, Bishopsgate, London.

~ The top court in the land hears a petition from London authorities to ban all stage plays.

~ Famine in Stratford is at its worst this winter.

{ 1597–8 }

SHAKESPEARE WRITES
★HENRY IV
(IN TWO PARTS)

1598

Thirty-four years old.

◆The Theatre is dismantled by Shakespeare's company (see pages 6–7).

◆For the first time, a play is published under Shakespeare's name: *Love's Labour's Lost.*

◆Shakespeare acts in *Every Man in His Humour,* a play by Ben Jonson.

◆Shakespeare is found to be hoarding grain, hoping that prices might rise.

◆Shakespeare invests in knitted stockings.

~ Opening of the first workhouses—places where unemployed people are sent to live.

~ English troops are defeated in Ireland.

{ 1598–9 }

SHAKESPEARE WRITES
★MUCH ADO ABOUT NOTHING
★HENRY V
★THE MERRY WIVES OF WINDSOR

1599

Thirty-five years old.

◆The Globe Theatre is built and opened on Bankside, Southwark.

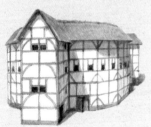

Shakespeare and other members of the Lord Chamberlain's Men own shares in it. *Julius Caesar* may be one of the first plays to be performed there.

◆Shakespeare is reported for not paying his taxes.

{ 1599–1600 }

SHAKESPEARE WRITES
★JULIUS CAESAR
★AS YOU LIKE IT
★TWELFTH NIGHT

1600

Thirty-six years old.

♦*Henry IV* **is performed at court.**

〜 There is bitter war in Ireland. Many royal woods are cut down to pay for it.

〜 The telescope is invented in Holland.

{ 1600–1 }

SHAKESPEARE WRITES
★HAMLET
★TROILUS AND CRESSIDA

1601

Thirty-seven years old.

♦**Shakespeare's father dies.**

♦**By special request from the Earl of Essex's supporters,** *Richard II* **(including some lines that Queen Elizabeth might have thought were treasonable) is performed at the Globe Theatre the day before Essex's rebellion. Essex is later beheaded.**

〜 Three thousand Spanish troops land in Ireland to fight the English.

1602

Thirty-eight years old.

♦**Shakespeare buys land and a cottage in Stratford.**

{ 1602–3 }

SHAKESPEARE WRITES
★ALL'S WELL THAT ENDS WELL
★OTHELLO

1603

Thirty-nine years old.

♦**The Lord Chamberlain's Men become the King's Men, with Shakespeare a prominent member.**

〜 Elizabeth I dies. James VI of Scotland is crowned James I of England.

〜 A petition is presented to the King with one thousand signatures from Puritans asking to abolish "ritual" in church services.

〜 Thirty thousand people die of the plague in London. The theatres are closed.

〜 Rebellion in Ireland is defeated by English troops.

〜 The first English bank is set up.

{ 1603–4 }

SHAKESPEARE WRITES
★MEASURE FOR MEASURE

1604

Forty years old.

〜 Peace with Spain.

{ 1604–5 }

SHAKESPEARE WRITES
★TIMON OF ATHENS

1605

Forty-one years old.

♦**Shakespeare buys the right to collect taxes (tithes) from people living near Stratford.**

♦ *Henry V* and *The Merchant of Venice* are **performed at court.**

〜 Guy Fawkes and others try to blow up the Houses of Parliament in the Gunpowder Plot.

{ 1605–6 }

SHAKESPEARE WRITES
★MACBETH
★KING LEAR

1606

Forty-two years old.

〜 A law is passed saying that Roman Catholics cannot hold public office.

〜 Portuguese explorers reach seas north of Australia.

{ 1606–7 }

SHAKESPEARE WRITES
★ANTONY AND CLEOPATRA

1607

Forty-three years old.

♦**Shakespeare's daughter Susanna marries Dr. John Hall in Stratford.**

♦**Shakespeare's brother Edmund dies.**

〜 Riots against common land being enclosed in Northamptonshire and Leicestershire.

〜 Flight of the northern earls from Ireland.

〜 Settlement of Virginia (now in the U.S.A.).

{ 1607–8 }

SHAKESPEARE WRITES
★CORIOLANUS

1608

Forty-four years old.

♦**Shakespeare's grand-daughter Elizabeth is born.**

♦**Shakespeare's mother, Mary, dies.**

{ 1608–9 }

SHAKESPEARE WRITES
★PERICLES

1609

Forty-five years old.

♦**Shakespeare's** *Sonnets* **are published.**

〜 English and Scots Protestants start settling in great numbers in northern Ireland.

〜 Tea arrives in Europe from China.

{ 1609–10 }

SHAKESPEARE WRITES
★CYMBELINE

1610

Forty-six years old.

♦ **Shakespeare returns to live in Stratford.**